1

This Journal belongs to:

Ruby-Jean Turner

Table of Contents

Goal 1	
Goal 2	

Weekly Check in

WEEK	DAY						
1	1	2	3	4	5	6	7
2	1	2	3	4	5	6	7
3	1	2	3	4	5	6	7
4	1	2	3	4	5	6	7
5	1	2	3	4	5	6	7
6	1	2	3	4	5	6	7
7	1	2	3	4	5	6	7
8	1	2	3	4	5	6	7
9	1	2	3	4	5	6	7
10	1	2	3	4	5	6	7
11	1	2	3	4	5	6	7
12	1	2	3	4	5	6	FIN

Start Date		End Date	
Start Weight		End Weight	

Week 1

Weight		
Neck		
Shoulders		
Chest		
Arms	Left	Right
Waist		
Hips		
Thighs	Left	Right
Calf	Left	Right

Meal Planner

MON	❑ Meal 1	❑ Meal 2	❑ Meal 3
TUE	❑ Meal 1	❑ Meal 2	❑ Meal 3
WED	❑ Meal 1	❑ Meal 2	❑ Meal 3
THU	❑ Meal 1 Porriage. + Strawberries.	❑ Meal 2 Ceasar Salad	☑ Meal 3 Carbonaro
FRI	❑ Meal 1	❑ Meal 2	❑ Meal 3
SAT	❑ Meal 1	❑ Meal 2	❑ Meal 3
SUN	❑ Meal 1	❑ Meal 2	❑ Meal 3

Exercise

Date:

Exercise	Reps	Sets
1. Sit ups	25	3
2. Squats	30	2
3. mountian climers	20	3
4. lunges	25	2
5. Calf raises	30	2
6. one leged squat	15	2
7. Crunches with legs up	25	3
8. Star jumps	30	4
9.		
10.		

Time

Location
- [ ] Gym
- [x] Home
- [x] Outdoors
- [ ] Aquatics
- [ ] Class
- [ ] Other

Focus
- [x] Cardio
- [ ] Toning
- [x] Strength
- [ ] Endurance
- [x] Fitness
- [ ] Maintenance
- [ ] Fat Burn
- [ ] Flexibility
- [ ] Other

Stretch Time

Distance/Steps

Intensity

Day off?	Supplements	Calories Burned	Exercise Mood

Food & Drink

Meal 1:

Time	Mood	Calories

Meal 2:

Time	Mood	Calories

Meal 3:

Time	Mood	Calories

Water & Drinks

Snack:

Time	Calories

Snack:

Time	Calories

Calories Eaten	Calories Burned	End of day Mood

Summary:

Exercise

Date:			
Exercise		**Reps**	**Sets**
1.			
2.			
3.			
4.			
5.			
6.			
7.			
8.			
9.			
10.			

Time

Location
- [ ] Gym
- [ ] Home
- [ ] Outdoors
- [ ] Aquatics
- [ ] Class
- [ ] Other

Focus
- [ ] Cardio
- [ ] Toning
- [ ] Strength
- [ ] Endurance
- [ ] Fitness
- [ ] Maintenance
- [ ] Fat Burn
- [ ] Flexibility
- [ ] Other

Stretch Time

Distance/Steps

Intensity

Day off?	Supplements	Calories Burned	Exercise Mood

Food & Drink

Meal 1:

Time	Mood	Calories

Meal 2:

Time	Mood	Calories

Meal 3:

Time	Mood	Calories

Water & Drinks

Snack:

Time	Calories

Snack:

Time	Calories

Calories Eaten	Calories Burned	End of day Mood

Summary:

Exercise

Date:

Exercise	Reps	Sets
1.		
2.		
3.		
4.		
5.		
6.		
7.		
8.		
9.		
10.		

Time

Location

- [ ] Gym
- [ ] Home
- [ ] Outdoors
- [ ] Aquatics
- [ ] Class
- [ ] Other

Focus

- [ ] Cardio
- [ ] Toning
- [ ] Strength
- [ ] Endurance
- [ ] Fitness
- [ ] Maintenance
- [ ] Fat Burn
- [ ] Flexibility
- [ ] Other

Stretch Time

Distance/Steps

Intensity

Day off?	Supplements	Calories Burned	Exercise Mood

Food & Drink

Meal 1:

Time	Mood	Calories

Meal 2:

Time	Mood	Calories

Meal 3:

Time	Mood	Calories

Water & Drinks

Snack:

Time	Calories

Snack:

Time	Calories

Calories Eaten	Calories Burned	End of day Mood

Summary:

Thursday 28th July

Exercise

Date:			
Exercise		**Reps**	**Sets**
1. 10 min Run.			
2. 5 min Skipping			
3. Kick ups.			
4. Dog Walk.			
5.			
6.			
7.			
8.			
9.			
10.			

Time

Location
- [ ] Gym
- [ ] Home
- [ ] Outdoors
- [ ] Aquatics
- [ ] Class
- [ ] Other

Focus
- [ ] Cardio
- [ ] Toning
- [ ] Strength
- [ ] Endurance
- [ ] Fitness
- [ ] Maintenance
- [ ] Fat Burn
- [ ] Flexibility
- [ ] Other

Stretch Time

Distance/Steps

Intensity

Day off?	Supplements	Calories Burned	Exercise Mood

Food & Drink

Meal 1:

Porriage + Strawberries.

Time	Mood	Calories

Meal 2:

Chicken
Cesear Salad

Time	Mood	Calories

Meal 3:

Carbinara.

Time	Mood	Calories

Water
&
Drinks

Snack:		Snack:	
Time	Calories	Time	Calories

Calories Eaten	Calories Burned	End of day Mood

Summary:

Friday 29th July . # Exercise

Date:

Exercise	Reps	Sets
1. Squats . x 30		
2. Jumping Squats x 15		
3. Reverse lunges x 20		
4. Side Squat x 15		
5. ~~Star Jump~~		
6. Calfs . x 25		
7. 1 legged squat x 10		
8.		
9.		
10.		

Time

Location
- [ ] Gym
- [ ] Home
- [ ] Outdoors
- [ ] Aquatics
- [ ] Class
- [ ] Other

Focus
- [ ] Cardio
- [ ] Toning
- [ ] Strength
- [ ] Endurance
- [ ] Fitness
- [ ] Maintenance
- [ ] Fat Burn
- [ ] Flexibility
- [ ] Other

Stretch Time

Distance/Steps

Intensity

Day off?	Supplements	Calories Burned	Exercise Mood

Food & Drink

Meal 1:

Time	Mood	Calories

Meal 2:

Time	Mood	Calories

Meal 3:

Time	Mood	Calories

Water & Drinks

Snack:

Time	Calories

Snack:

Time	Calories

Calories Eaten	Calories Burned	End of day Mood

Summary:

_____

_____

_____

Saturday 30th July # Exercise

Date:		
Exercise	**Reps**	**Sets**
1. Football Training		
2.		
3.		
4.		
5.		
6.		
7.		
8.		
9.		
10.		

Time

Location
- [ ] Gym
- [ ] Home
- [ ] Outdoors
- [ ] Aquatics
- [ ] Class
- [ ] Other

Focus
- [ ] Cardio
- [ ] Toning
- [ ] Strength
- [ ] Endurance
- [ ] Fitness
- [ ] Maintenance
- [ ] Fat Burn
- [ ] Flexibility
- [ ] Other

Stretch Time

Distance/Steps

Intensity

Day off?	Supplements	Calories Burned	Exercise Mood

18

Food & Drink

Meal 1:

Time	Mood	Calories

Meal 2:

Time	Mood	Calories

Meal 3:

Time	Mood	Calories

Water & Drinks

Snack:

Snack:

Time	Calories	Time	Calories

Calories Eaten	Calories Burned	End of day Mood

Summary:

Exercise

Date:

	Exercise	Reps	Sets
1.			
2.			
3.			
4.			
5.			
6.			
7.			
8.			
9.			
10.			

Time

Location
- [ ] Gym
- [ ] Home
- [ ] Outdoors
- [ ] Aquatics
- [ ] Class
- [ ] Other

Focus
- [ ] Cardio
- [ ] Toning
- [ ] Strength
- [ ] Endurance
- [ ] Fitness
- [ ] Maintenance
- [ ] Fat Burn
- [ ] Flexibility
- [ ] Other

Stretch Time

Distance/Steps

Intensity

Day off?	Supplements	Calories Burned	Exercise Mood

Food & Drink

Meal 1:

Time	Mood	Calories

Meal 2:

Time	Mood	Calories

Meal 3:

Time	Mood	Calories

Water & Drinks

Snack:

Time	Calories

Snack:

Time	Calories

Calories Eaten	Calories Burned	End of day Mood

Summary:

_____

_____

_____

_____

Week 2

Meal Planner

MON	❑ Meal 1	❑ Meal 2	❑ Meal 3
TUE	❑ Meal 1	❑ Meal 2	❑ Meal 3
WED	❑ Meal 1	❑ Meal 2	❑ Meal 3
THU	❑ Meal 1	❑ Meal 2	❑ Meal 3
FRI	❑ Meal 1	❑ Meal 2	❑ Meal 3
SAT	❑ Meal 1	❑ Meal 2	❑ Meal 3
SUN	❑ Meal 1	❑ Meal 2	❑ Meal 3

Exercise

Date:

Exercise	Reps	Sets
1.		
2.		
3.		
4.		
5.		
6.		
7.		
8.		
9.		
10.		

Time

Location
- [ ] Gym
- [ ] Home
- [ ] Outdoors
- [ ] Aquatics
- [ ] Class
- [ ] Other

Focus
- [ ] Cardio
- [ ] Toning
- [ ] Strength
- [ ] Endurance
- [ ] Fitness
- [ ] Maintenance
- [ ] Fat Burn
- [ ] Flexibility
- [ ] Other

Stretch Time

Distance/Steps

Intensity

Day off?	Supplements	Calories Burned	Exercise Mood

Food & Drink

Meal 1:

Time	Mood	Calories

Meal 2:

Time	Mood	Calories

Meal 3:

Time	Mood	Calories

Water & Drinks

Snack:

Time	Calories

Snack:

Time	Calories

Calories Eaten	Calories Burned	End of day Mood

Summary:

Exercise

Date:

Exercise	Reps	Sets
1.		
2.		
3.		
4.		
5.		
6.		
7.		
8.		
9.		
10.		

Time

Location
- [ ] Gym
- [ ] Home
- [ ] Outdoors
- [ ] Aquatics
- [ ] Class
- [ ] Other

Focus
- [ ] Cardio
- [ ] Toning
- [ ] Strength
- [ ] Endurance
- [ ] Fitness
- [ ] Maintenance
- [ ] Fat Burn
- [ ] Flexibility
- [ ] Other

Stretch Time

Distance/Steps

Intensity

Day off?	Supplements	Calories Burned	Exercise Mood

Food & Drink

Meal 1:

Time	Mood	Calories

Meal 2:

Time	Mood	Calories

Meal 3:

Time	Mood	Calories

Water & Drinks

Snack:

Time	Calories

Snack:

Time	Calories

Calories Eaten	Calories Burned	End of day Mood

Summary:

Exercise

Date:

Exercise	Reps	Sets
1.		
2.		
3.		
4.		
5.		
6.		
7.		
8.		
9.		
10.		

Time

Location
- [ ] Gym
- [ ] Home
- [ ] Outdoors
- [ ] Aquatics
- [ ] Class
- [ ] Other

Focus
- [ ] Cardio
- [ ] Toning
- [ ] Strength
- [ ] Endurance
- [ ] Fitness
- [ ] Maintenance
- [ ] Fat Burn
- [ ] Flexibility
- [ ] Other

Stretch Time

Distance/Steps

Intensity

Day off?	Supplements	Calories Burned	Exercise Mood

28

Food & Drink

Meal 1:

Time	Mood	Calories

Meal 2:

Time	Mood	Calories

Meal 3:

Time	Mood	Calories

Water & Drinks

Snack:

Time	Calories

Snack:

Time	Calories

Calories Eaten	Calories Burned	End of day Mood

Summary:

_____

_____

_____

Exercise

Date:

Exercise	Reps	Sets
1.		
2.		
3.		
4.		
5.		
6.		
7.		
8.		
9.		
10.		

Time

Location
- [ ] Gym
- [ ] Home
- [ ] Outdoors
- [ ] Aquatics
- [ ] Class
- [ ] Other

Focus
- [ ] Cardio
- [ ] Toning
- [ ] Strength
- [ ] Endurance
- [ ] Fitness
- [ ] Maintenance
- [ ] Fat Burn
- [ ] Flexibility
- [ ] Other

Stretch Time

Distance/Steps

Intensity

Day off?	Supplements	Calories Burned	Exercise Mood

Food & Drink

Meal 1:

Time	Mood	Calories

Meal 2:

Time	Mood	Calories

Meal 3:

Time	Mood	Calories

Snack:		Snack:	
Time	Calories	Time	Calories

Water & Drinks

Calories Eaten	Calories Burned	End of day Mood

Summary:

Exercise

Date:

Exercise	Reps	Sets
1.		
2.		
3.		
4.		
5.		
6.		
7.		
8.		
9.		
10.		

Time

Location
☐ Gym
☐ Home
☐ Outdoors
☐ Aquatics
☐ Class
☐ Other

Focus
☐ Cardio
☐ Toning
☐ Strength
☐ Endurance
☐ Fitness
☐ Maintenance
☐ Fat Burn
☐ Flexibility
☐ Other

Stretch Time

Distance/Steps

Intensity

Day off?	Supplements	Calories Burned	Exercise Mood

Food & Drink

Meal 1:

Time	Mood	Calories

Meal 2:

Time	Mood	Calories

Meal 3:

Time	Mood	Calories

Water & Drinks

Snack:		Snack:	
Time	Calories	Time	Calories

Calories Eaten	Calories Burned	End of day Mood

Summary:

Exercise

Date:		
Exercise	**Reps**	**Sets**
1.		
2.		
3.		
4.		
5.		
6.		
7.		
8.		
9.		
10.		

Time

Location
- [ ] Gym
- [ ] Home
- [ ] Outdoors
- [ ] Aquatics
- [ ] Class
- [ ] Other

Focus
- [ ] Cardio
- [ ] Toning
- [ ] Strength
- [ ] Endurance
- [ ] Fitness
- [ ] Maintenance
- [ ] Fat Burn
- [ ] Flexibility
- [ ] Other

Stretch Time

Distance/Steps

Intensity

Day off?	Supplements	Calories Burned	Exercise Mood

Food & Drink

Meal 1:

Time	Mood	Calories

Meal 2:

Time	Mood	Calories

Meal 3:

Time	Mood	Calories

Water & Drinks

Snack:

Time	Calories

Snack:

Time	Calories

Calories Eaten	Calories Burned	End of day Mood

Summary:

Exercise

Date:		
Exercise	**Reps**	**Sets**
1.		
2.		
3.		
4.		
5.		
6.		
7.		
8.		
9.		
10.		

Time

Location
- ☐ Gym
- ☐ Home
- ☐ Outdoors
- ☐ Aquatics
- ☐ Class
- ☐ Other

Focus
- ☐ Cardio
- ☐ Toning
- ☐ Strength
- ☐ Endurance
- ☐ Fitness
- ☐ Maintenance
- ☐ Fat Burn
- ☐ Flexibility
- ☐ Other

Stretch Time

Distance/Steps

Intensity

Day off?	Supplements	Calories Burned	Exercise Mood

Food & Drink

Meal 1:

Time	Mood	Calories

Meal 2:

Time	Mood	Calories

Meal 3:

Time	Mood	Calories

Water & Drinks

Snack:		Snack:	
Time	Calories	Time	Calories

Calories Eaten	Calories Burned	End of day Mood

Summary:

Week 3

Meal Planner

MON	☐ Meal 1	☐ Meal 2	☐ Meal 3
TUE	☐ Meal 1	☐ Meal 2	☐ Meal 3
WED	☐ Meal 1	☐ Meal 2	☐ Meal 3
THU	☐ Meal 1	☐ Meal 2	☐ Meal 3
FRI	☐ Meal 1	☐ Meal 2	☐ Meal 3
SAT	☐ Meal 1	☐ Meal 2	☐ Meal 3
SUN	☐ Meal 1	☐ Meal 2	☐ Meal 3

Exercise

Date:

Exercise	Reps	Sets
1.		
2.		
3.		
4.		
5.		
6.		
7.		
8.		
9.		
10.		

Time

Location
- [ ] Gym
- [ ] Home
- [ ] Outdoors
- [ ] Aquatics
- [ ] Class
- [ ] Other

Focus
- [ ] Cardio
- [ ] Toning
- [ ] Strength
- [ ] Endurance
- [ ] Fitness
- [ ] Maintenance
- [ ] Fat Burn
- [ ] Flexibility
- [ ] Other

Stretch Time

Distance/Steps

Intensity

Day off?	Supplements	Calories Burned	Exercise Mood

Food & Drink

Meal 1:

Time	Mood	Calories

Meal 2:

Time	Mood	Calories

Meal 3:

Time	Mood	Calories

Water & Drinks

Snack: | **Snack:**

Time	Calories	Time	Calories

Calories Eaten	Calories Burned	End of day Mood

Summary:

Exercise

Date:

Exercise	Reps	Sets
1.		
2.		
3.		
4.		
5.		
6.		
7.		
8.		
9.		
10.		

Time

Location

- [ ] Gym
- [ ] Home
- [ ] Outdoors
- [ ] Aquatics
- [ ] Class
- [ ] Other

Focus

- [ ] Cardio
- [ ] Toning
- [ ] Strength
- [ ] Endurance
- [ ] Fitness
- [ ] Maintenance
- [ ] Fat Burn
- [ ] Flexibility
- [ ] Other

Stretch Time

Distance/Steps

Intensity

Day off?	Supplements	Calories Burned	Exercise Mood

Food & Drink

Meal 1:

Time	Mood	Calories

Meal 2:

Time	Mood	Calories

Meal 3:

Time	Mood	Calories

Water & Drinks

Snack:		Snack:	
Time	Calories	Time	Calories

Calories Eaten	Calories Burned	End of day Mood

Summary:

_____

_____

_____

Exercise

Date:

Exercise	Reps	Sets
1.		
2.		
3.		
4.		
5.		
6.		
7.		
8.		
9.		
10.		

Time

Location

- ☐ Gym
- ☐ Home
- ☐ Outdoors
- ☐ Aquatics
- ☐ Class
- ☐ Other

Focus

- ☐ Cardio
- ☐ Toning
- ☐ Strength
- ☐ Endurance
- ☐ Fitness
- ☐ Maintenance
- ☐ Fat Burn
- ☐ Flexibility
- ☐ Other

Stretch Time

Distance/Steps

Intensity

Day off?	Supplements	Calories Burned	Exercise Mood

Food & Drink

Meal 1:

Time	Mood	Calories

Meal 2:

Time	Mood	Calories

Meal 3:

Time	Mood	Calories

Water & Drinks

Snack:

Time	Calories

Snack:

Time	Calories

Calories Eaten	Calories Burned	End of day Mood

Summary:

Exercise

Date:

Exercise	Reps	Sets
1.		
2.		
3.		
4.		
5.		
6.		
7.		
8.		
9.		
10.		

Time

Location
- [ ] Gym
- [ ] Home
- [ ] Outdoors
- [ ] Aquatics
- [ ] Class
- [ ] Other

Focus
- [ ] Cardio
- [ ] Toning
- [ ] Strength
- [ ] Endurance
- [ ] Fitness
- [ ] Maintenance
- [ ] Fat Burn
- [ ] Flexibility
- [ ] Other

Stretch Time

Distance/Steps

Intensity

Day off?	Supplements	Calories Burned	Exercise Mood

Food & Drink

Meal 1:

Time	Mood	Calories

Meal 2:

Time	Mood	Calories

Meal 3:

Time	Mood	Calories

Water & Drinks

Snack:		Snack:	
Time	Calories	Time	Calories

Calories Eaten	Calories Burned	End of day Mood

Summary:

Exercise

Date:

Exercise	Reps	Sets
1.		
2.		
3.		
4.		
5.		
6.		
7.		
8.		
9.		
10.		

Time

Location

- [ ] Gym
- [ ] Home
- [ ] Outdoors
- [ ] Aquatics
- [ ] Class
- [ ] Other

Focus

- [ ] Cardio
- [ ] Toning
- [ ] Strength
- [ ] Endurance
- [ ] Fitness
- [ ] Maintenance
- [ ] Fat Burn
- [ ] Flexibility
- [ ] Other

Stretch Time

Distance/Steps

Intensity

Day off?	Supplements	Calories Burned	Exercise Mood

Food & Drink

Meal 1:

Time	Mood	Calories

Meal 2:

Time	Mood	Calories

Meal 3:

Time	Mood	Calories

Water & Drinks

Snack:

Snack:

Time	Calories	Time	Calories

Calories Eaten	Calories Burned	End of day Mood

Summary:

Exercise

Date:

Exercise	Reps	Sets
1.		
2.		
3.		
4.		
5.		
6.		
7.		
8.		
9.		
10.		

Time

Location

- [ ] Gym
- [ ] Home
- [ ] Outdoors
- [ ] Aquatics
- [ ] Class
- [ ] Other

Focus

- [ ] Cardio
- [ ] Toning
- [ ] Strength
- [ ] Endurance
- [ ] Fitness
- [ ] Maintenance
- [ ] Fat Burn
- [ ] Flexibility
- [ ] Other

Stretch Time

Distance/Steps

Intensity

Day off?	Supplements	Calories Burned	Exercise Mood

Food & Drink

Meal 1:

Time	Mood	Calories

Meal 2:

Time	Mood	Calories

Meal 3:

Time	Mood	Calories

Water & Drinks

Snack:		Snack:	
Time	Calories	Time	Calories

Calories Eaten	Calories Burned	End of day Mood

Summary:

Exercise

Date:

Exercise	Reps	Sets
1.		
2.		
3.		
4.		
5.		
6.		
7.		
8.		
9.		
10.		

Time

Location
- [ ] Gym
- [ ] Home
- [ ] Outdoors
- [ ] Aquatics
- [ ] Class
- [ ] Other

Focus
- [ ] Cardio
- [ ] Toning
- [ ] Strength
- [ ] Endurance
- [ ] Fitness
- [ ] Maintenance
- [ ] Fat Burn
- [ ] Flexibility
- [ ] Other

Stretch Time

Distance/Steps

Intensity

Day off?	Supplements	Calories Burned	Exercise Mood

Food & Drink

Meal 1:

Time	Mood	Calories

Meal 2:

Time	Mood	Calories

Meal 3:

Time	Mood	Calories

Water & Drinks

Snack:

Time	Calories

Snack:

Time	Calories

Calories Eaten	Calories Burned	End of day Mood

Summary:

Week 4

Weight		
Neck		
Shoulders		
Chest		
Arms	Left	Right
Waist		
Hips		
Thighs	Left	Right
Calf	Left	Right

Meal Planner

MON	☐ Meal 1	☐ Meal 2	☐ Meal 3
TUE	☐ Meal 1	☐ Meal 2	☐ Meal 3
WED	☐ Meal 1	☐ Meal 2	☐ Meal 3
THU	☐ Meal 1	☐ Meal 2	☐ Meal 3
FRI	☐ Meal 1	☐ Meal 2	☐ Meal 3
SAT	☐ Meal 1	☐ Meal 2	☐ Meal 3
SUN	☐ Meal 1	☐ Meal 2	☐ Meal 3

Exercise

Date:

Exercise	Reps	Sets
1.		
2.		
3.		
4.		
5.		
6.		
7.		
8.		
9.		
10.		

Time

Location
- [ ] Gym
- [ ] Home
- [ ] Outdoors
- [ ] Aquatics
- [ ] Class
- [ ] Other

Focus
- [ ] Cardio
- [ ] Toning
- [ ] Strength
- [ ] Endurance
- [ ] Fitness
- [ ] Maintenance
- [ ] Fat Burn
- [ ] Flexibility
- [ ] Other

Stretch Time

Distance/Steps

Intensity

Day off?	Supplements	Calories Burned	Exercise Mood

Food & Drink

Meal 1:

Time	Mood	Calories

Meal 2:

Time	Mood	Calories

Meal 3:

Time	Mood	Calories

Water & Drinks

Snack:		Snack:	
Time	Calories	Time	Calories

Calories Eaten	Calories Burned	End of day Mood

Summary:

Exercise

Date:

	Exercise	Reps	Sets
1.			
2.			
3.			
4.			
5.			
6.			
7.			
8.			
9.			
10.			

Time

Location
- [ ] Gym
- [ ] Home
- [ ] Outdoors
- [ ] Aquatics
- [ ] Class
- [ ] Other

Focus
- [ ] Cardio
- [ ] Toning
- [ ] Strength
- [ ] Endurance
- [ ] Fitness
- [ ] Maintenance
- [ ] Fat Burn
- [ ] Flexibility
- [ ] Other

Stretch Time

Distance/Steps

Intensity

Day off?	Supplements	Calories Burned	Exercise Mood

Food & Drink

Meal 1:

Time	Mood	Calories

Meal 2:

Time	Mood	Calories

Meal 3:

Time	Mood	Calories

Water & Drinks

Snack:

Time	Calories

Snack:

Time	Calories

Calories Eaten	Calories Burned	End of day Mood

Summary:

Exercise

Date:

	Exercise	Reps	Sets
1.			
2.			
3.			
4.			
5.			
6.			
7.			
8.			
9.			
10.			

Time

Location
- ☐ Gym
- ☐ Home
- ☐ Outdoors
- ☐ Aquatics
- ☐ Class
- ☐ Other

Focus
- ☐ Cardio
- ☐ Toning
- ☐ Strength
- ☐ Endurance
- ☐ Fitness
- ☐ Maintenance
- ☐ Fat Burn
- ☐ Flexibility
- ☐ Other

Stretch Time

Distance/Steps

Intensity

Day off?	Supplements	Calories Burned	Exercise Mood

Food & Drink

Meal 1:

Time	Mood	Calories

Meal 2:

Time	Mood	Calories

Meal 3:

Time	Mood	Calories

Water & Drinks

Snack:		Snack:	
Time	Calories	Time	Calories

Calories Eaten	Calories Burned	End of day Mood

Summary:

_____

_____

_____

Exercise

Date:

Exercise	Reps	Sets
1.		
2.		
3.		
4.		
5.		
6.		
7.		
8.		
9.		
10.		

Time

Location

- [ ] Gym
- [ ] Home
- [ ] Outdoors
- [ ] Aquatics
- [ ] Class
- [ ] Other

Focus

- [ ] Cardio
- [ ] Toning
- [ ] Strength
- [ ] Endurance
- [ ] Fitness
- [ ] Maintenance
- [ ] Fat Burn
- [ ] Flexibility
- [ ] Other

Stretch Time

Distance/Steps

Intensity

Day off?	Supplements	Calories Burned	Exercise Mood

Food & Drink

Meal 1:

Time	Mood	Calories

Meal 2:

Time	Mood	Calories

Meal 3:

Time	Mood	Calories

Snack:		Snack:	
Time	Calories	Time	Calories

Water & Drinks

Calories Eaten	Calories Burned	End of day Mood

Summary:

Exercise

Date:

	Exercise	Reps	Sets
1.			
2.			
3.			
4.			
5.			
6.			
7.			
8.			
9.			
10.			

Time

Location
- [ ] Gym
- [ ] Home
- [ ] Outdoors
- [ ] Aquatics
- [ ] Class
- [ ] Other

Focus
- [ ] Cardio
- [ ] Toning
- [ ] Strength
- [ ] Endurance
- [ ] Fitness
- [ ] Maintenance
- [ ] Fat Burn
- [ ] Flexibility
- [ ] Other

Stretch Time

Distance/Steps

Intensity

Day off?	Supplements	Calories Burned	Exercise Mood

Food & Drink

Meal 1:

Time	Mood	Calories

Meal 2:

Time	Mood	Calories

Meal 3:

Time	Mood	Calories

Water & Drinks

Snack:

Snack:

Time	Calories	Time	Calories

Calories Eaten	Calories Burned	End of day Mood

Summary: _____

_____

_____

_____

Exercise

Date:

	Exercise	Reps	Sets
1.			
2.			
3.			
4.			
5.			
6.			
7.			
8.			
9.			
10.			

Time

Location
- [ ] Gym
- [ ] Home
- [ ] Outdoors
- [ ] Aquatics
- [ ] Class
- [ ] Other

Focus
- [ ] Cardio
- [ ] Toning
- [ ] Strength
- [ ] Endurance
- [ ] Fitness
- [ ] Maintenance
- [ ] Fat Burn
- [ ] Flexibility
- [ ] Other

Stretch Time

Distance/Steps

Intensity

Day off?	Supplements		Calories Burned	Exercise Mood

Food & Drink

Meal 1:

Time	Mood	Calories

Meal 2:

Time	Mood	Calories

Meal 3:

Time	Mood	Calories

Water & Drinks

Snack:

Time	Calories

Snack:

Time	Calories

Calories Eaten	Calories Burned	End of day Mood

Summary:

Exercise

Date:

Exercise	Reps	Sets
1.		
2.		
3.		
4.		
5.		
6.		
7.		
8.		
9.		
10.		

Time

Location
- [ ] Gym
- [ ] Home
- [ ] Outdoors
- [ ] Aquatics
- [ ] Class
- [ ] Other

Focus
- [ ] Cardio
- [ ] Toning
- [ ] Strength
- [ ] Endurance
- [ ] Fitness
- [ ] Maintenance
- [ ] Fat Burn
- [ ] Flexibility
- [ ] Other

Stretch Time

Distance/Steps

Intensity

Day off?	Supplements	Calories Burned	Exercise Mood

Food & Drink

Meal 1:

Time	Mood	Calories

Meal 2:

Time	Mood	Calories

Meal 3:

Time	Mood	Calories

Water & Drinks

Snack:		Snack:	
Time	Calories	Time	Calories

Calories Eaten	Calories Burned	End of day Mood

Summary:

Week 5

Meal Planner

MON	❑ Meal 1	❑ Meal 2	❑ Meal 3
TUE	❑ Meal 1	❑ Meal 2	❑ Meal 3
WED	❑ Meal 1	❑ Meal 2	❑ Meal 3
THU	❑ Meal 1	❑ Meal 2	❑ Meal 3
FRI	❑ Meal 1	❑ Meal 2	❑ Meal 3
SAT	❑ Meal 1	❑ Meal 2	❑ Meal 3
SUN	❑ Meal 1	❑ Meal 2	❑ Meal 3

Exercise

Date:

Exercise	Reps	Sets
1.		
2.		
3.		
4.		
5.		
6.		
7.		
8.		
9.		
10.		

Time

Location

- [ ] Gym
- [ ] Home
- [ ] Outdoors
- [ ] Aquatics
- [ ] Class
- [ ] Other

Focus

- [ ] Cardio
- [ ] Toning
- [ ] Strength
- [ ] Endurance
- [ ] Fitness
- [ ] Maintenance
- [ ] Fat Burn
- [ ] Flexibility
- [ ] Other

Stretch Time

Distance/Steps

Intensity

Day off?	Supplements	Calories Burned	Exercise Mood

72

Food & Drink

Meal 1:

Time	Mood	Calories

Meal 2:

Time	Mood	Calories

Meal 3:

Time	Mood	Calories

Water & Drinks

Snack:

Time	Calories

Snack:

Time	Calories

Calories Eaten	Calories Burned	End of day Mood

Summary:

Exercise

Date:

Exercise	Reps	Sets
1.		
2.		
3.		
4.		
5.		
6.		
7.		
8.		
9.		
10.		

Time

Location
- [ ] Gym
- [ ] Home
- [ ] Outdoors
- [ ] Aquatics
- [ ] Class
- [ ] Other

Focus
- [ ] Cardio
- [ ] Toning
- [ ] Strength
- [ ] Endurance
- [ ] Fitness
- [ ] Maintenance
- [ ] Fat Burn
- [ ] Flexibility
- [ ] Other

Stretch Time

Distance/Steps

Intensity

Day off?	Supplements	Calories Burned	Exercise Mood

Food & Drink

Meal 1:

Time	Mood	Calories

Meal 2:

Time	Mood	Calories

Meal 3:

Time	Mood	Calories

Water & Drinks

Snack:

Snack:

Time	Calories	Time	Calories

Calories Eaten	Calories Burned	End of day Mood

Summary:

Exercise

Date:		

Exercise	Reps	Sets
1.		
2.		
3.		
4.		
5.		
6.		
7.		
8.		
9.		
10.		

Time

Location

- [ ] Gym
- [ ] Home
- [ ] Outdoors
- [ ] Aquatics
- [ ] Class
- [ ] Other

Focus

- [ ] Cardio
- [ ] Toning
- [ ] Strength
- [ ] Endurance
- [ ] Fitness
- [ ] Maintenance
- [ ] Fat Burn
- [ ] Flexibility
- [ ] Other

Stretch Time

Distance/Steps

Intensity

Day off?	Supplements	Calories Burned	Exercise Mood

Food & Drink

Meal 1:

Time	Mood	Calories

Meal 2:

Time	Mood	Calories

Meal 3:

Time	Mood	Calories

Water & Drinks

Snack:		Snack:	
Time	Calories	Time	Calories

Calories Eaten	Calories Burned	End of day Mood

Summary:

Exercise

Date:

Exercise	Reps	Sets
1.		
2.		
3.		
4.		
5.		
6.		
7.		
8.		
9.		
10.		

Time

Location
- [ ] Gym
- [ ] Home
- [ ] Outdoors
- [ ] Aquatics
- [ ] Class
- [ ] Other

Focus
- [ ] Cardio
- [ ] Toning
- [ ] Strength
- [ ] Endurance
- [ ] Fitness
- [ ] Maintenance
- [ ] Fat Burn
- [ ] Flexibility
- [ ] Other

Stretch Time

Distance/Steps

Intensity

Day off?	Supplements	Calories Burned	Exercise Mood

Food & Drink

Meal 1:

Time	Mood	Calories

Meal 2:

Time	Mood	Calories

Meal 3:

Time	Mood	Calories

Water & Drinks

Snack: | Snack:

Time	Calories	Time	Calories

Calories Eaten	Calories Burned	End of day Mood

Summary:

Exercise

Date:

Exercise	Reps	Sets
1.		
2.		
3.		
4.		
5.		
6.		
7.		
8.		
9.		
10.		

Time

Location
- [ ] Gym
- [ ] Home
- [ ] Outdoors
- [ ] Aquatics
- [ ] Class
- [ ] Other

Focus
- [ ] Cardio
- [ ] Toning
- [ ] Strength
- [ ] Endurance
- [ ] Fitness
- [ ] Maintenance
- [ ] Fat Burn
- [ ] Flexibility
- [ ] Other

Stretch Time

Distance/Steps

Intensity

Day off?	Supplements	Calories Burned	Exercise Mood

Food & Drink

Meal 1:

Time	Mood	Calories

Meal 2:

Time	Mood	Calories

Meal 3:

Time	Mood	Calories

Water & Drinks

Snack: | | **Snack:** |

Time	Calories	Time	Calories

Calories Eaten	Calories Burned	End of day Mood

Summary:

Exercise

Date:

Exercise	Reps	Sets
1.		
2.		
3.		
4.		
5.		
6.		
7.		
8.		
9.		
10.		

Time

Location
- [ ] Gym
- [ ] Home
- [ ] Outdoors
- [ ] Aquatics
- [ ] Class
- [ ] Other

Focus
- [ ] Cardio
- [ ] Toning
- [ ] Strength
- [ ] Endurance
- [ ] Fitness
- [ ] Maintenance
- [ ] Fat Burn
- [ ] Flexibility
- [ ] Other

Stretch Time

Distance/Steps

Intensity

Day off?	Supplements

Calories Burned	Exercise Mood

Food & Drink

Meal 1:

Time	Mood	Calories

Meal 2:

Time	Mood	Calories

Meal 3:

Time	Mood	Calories

Water & Drinks

Snack:		Snack:	
Time	Calories	Time	Calories

Calories Eaten	Calories Burned	End of day Mood

Summary:

Exercise

Date:

	Exercise	Reps	Sets
1.			
2.			
3.			
4.			
5.			
6.			
7.			
8.			
9.			
10.			

Time

Location
- ☐ Gym
- ☐ Home
- ☐ Outdoors
- ☐ Aquatics
- ☐ Class
- ☐ Other

Focus
- ☐ Cardio
- ☐ Toning
- ☐ Strength
- ☐ Endurance
- ☐ Fitness
- ☐ Maintenance
- ☐ Fat Burn
- ☐ Flexibility
- ☐ Other

Stretch Time

Distance/Steps

Intensity

Day off?	Supplements	Calories Burned	Exercise Mood

Food & Drink

Meal 1:

Time	Mood	Calories

Meal 2:

Time	Mood	Calories

Meal 3:

Time	Mood	Calories

Snack:		Snack:	
Time	Calories	Time	Calories

Water & Drinks

Calories Eaten	Calories Burned	End of day Mood

Summary:

Week 6

Meal Planner

MON	❑ Meal 1 ❑ Meal 2 ❑ Meal 3	
TUE	❑ Meal 1 ❑ Meal 2 ❑ Meal 3	
WED	❑ Meal 1 ❑ Meal 2 ❑ Meal 3	
THU	❑ Meal 1 ❑ Meal 2 ❑ Meal 3	
FRI	❑ Meal 1 ❑ Meal 2 ❑ Meal 3	
SAT	❑ Meal 1 ❑ Meal 2 ❑ Meal 3	
SUN	❑ Meal 1 ❑ Meal 2 ❑ Meal 3	

Exercise

	Exercise	Reps	Sets
1.			
2.			
3.			
4.			
5.			
6.			
7.			
8.			
9.			
10.			

Date:

Time

Location
- [ ] Gym
- [ ] Home
- [ ] Outdoors
- [ ] Aquatics
- [ ] Class
- [ ] Other

Focus
- [ ] Cardio
- [ ] Toning
- [ ] Strength
- [ ] Endurance
- [ ] Fitness
- [ ] Maintenance
- [ ] Fat Burn
- [ ] Flexibility
- [ ] Other

Stretch Time

Distance/Steps

Intensity

Day off?	Supplements	Calories Burned	Exercise Mood

Food & Drink

Meal 1:

Time	Mood	Calories

Meal 2:

Time	Mood	Calories

Meal 3:

Time	Mood	Calories

Water & Drinks

Snack:		Snack:	
Time	Calories	Time	Calories

Calories Eaten	Calories Burned	End of day Mood

Summary:

_____

_____

_____

_____

Exercise

Date:

Exercise	Reps	Sets
1.		
2.		
3.		
4.		
5.		
6.		
7.		
8.		
9.		
10.		

Time

Location
- [ ] Gym
- [ ] Home
- [ ] Outdoors
- [ ] Aquatics
- [ ] Class
- [ ] Other

Focus
- [ ] Cardio
- [ ] Toning
- [ ] Strength
- [ ] Endurance
- [ ] Fitness
- [ ] Maintenance
- [ ] Fat Burn
- [ ] Flexibility
- [ ] Other

Stretch Time

Distance/Steps

Intensity

Day off?	Supplements	Calories Burned	Exercise Mood

Food & Drink

Meal 1:

Time	Mood	Calories

Meal 2:

Time	Mood	Calories

Meal 3:

Time	Mood	Calories

Water & Drinks

Snack:		Snack:	
Time	Calories	Time	Calories

Calories Eaten	Calories Burned	End of day Mood

Summary:

Exercise

Date:

	Exercise	Reps	Sets
1.			
2.			
3.			
4.			
5.			
6.			
7.			
8.			
9.			
10.			

Time

Location
- [ ] Gym
- [ ] Home
- [ ] Outdoors
- [ ] Aquatics
- [ ] Class
- [ ] Other

Focus
- [ ] Cardio
- [ ] Toning
- [ ] Strength
- [ ] Endurance
- [ ] Fitness
- [ ] Maintenance
- [ ] Fat Burn
- [ ] Flexibility
- [ ] Other

Stretch Time

Distance/Steps

Intensity

Day off?	Supplements	Calories Burned	Exercise Mood

92

Food & Drink

Meal 1:

Time	Mood	Calories

Meal 2:

Time	Mood	Calories

Meal 3:

Time	Mood	Calories

Water & Drinks

Snack:		Snack:	
Time	Calories	Time	Calories

Calories Eaten	Calories Burned	End of day Mood

Summary:

Exercise

Date:

Exercise	Reps	Sets
1.		
2.		
3.		
4.		
5.		
6.		
7.		
8.		
9.		
10.		

Time

Location
- [ ] Gym
- [ ] Home
- [ ] Outdoors
- [ ] Aquatics
- [ ] Class
- [ ] Other

Focus
- [ ] Cardio
- [ ] Toning
- [ ] Strength
- [ ] Endurance
- [ ] Fitness
- [ ] Maintenance
- [ ] Fat Burn
- [ ] Flexibility
- [ ] Other

Stretch Time

Distance/Steps

Intensity

Day off?	Supplements	Calories Burned	Exercise Mood

Food & Drink

Meal 1:

Time	Mood	Calories

Meal 2:

Time	Mood	Calories

Meal 3:

Time	Mood	Calories

Water & Drinks

Snack:

Snack:

Time	Calories	Time	Calories

Calories Eaten	Calories Burned	End of day Mood

Summary:

Exercise

Date:

Exercise	Reps	Sets
1.		
2.		
3.		
4.		
5.		
6.		
7.		
8.		
9.		
10.		

Time

Location

- [ ] Gym
- [ ] Home
- [ ] Outdoors
- [ ] Aquatics
- [ ] Class
- [ ] Other

Focus

- [ ] Cardio
- [ ] Toning
- [ ] Strength
- [ ] Endurance
- [ ] Fitness
- [ ] Maintenance
- [ ] Fat Burn
- [ ] Flexibility
- [ ] Other

Stretch Time

Distance/Steps

Intensity

Day off?	Supplements	Calories Burned	Exercise Mood

Food & Drink

Meal 1:

Time	Mood	Calories

Meal 2:

Time	Mood	Calories

Meal 3:

Time	Mood	Calories

Water & Drinks

Snack:		Snack:	
Time	Calories	Time	Calories

Calories Eaten	Calories Burned	End of day Mood

Summary:

Exercise

Date:

	Exercise	Reps	Sets
1.			
2.			
3.			
4.			
5.			
6.			
7.			
8.			
9.			
10.			

Time

Location

- [ ] Gym
- [ ] Home
- [ ] Outdoors
- [ ] Aquatics
- [ ] Class
- [ ] Other

Focus

- [ ] Cardio
- [ ] Toning
- [ ] Strength
- [ ] Endurance
- [ ] Fitness
- [ ] Maintenance
- [ ] Fat Burn
- [ ] Flexibility
- [ ] Other

Stretch Time

Distance/Steps

Intensity

Day off?	Supplements	Calories Burned	Exercise Mood

Food & Drink

Meal 1:

Time	Mood	Calories

Meal 2:

Time	Mood	Calories

Meal 3:

Time	Mood	Calories

Water & Drinks

Snack:

Snack:

Time	Calories	Time	Calories

Calories Eaten	Calories Burned	End of day Mood

Summary:

Exercise

Date:		
Exercise	**Reps**	**Sets**
1.		
2.		
3.		
4.		
5.		
6.		
7.		
8.		
9.		
10.		

Time

Location
- [ ] Gym
- [ ] Home
- [ ] Outdoors
- [ ] Aquatics
- [ ] Class
- [ ] Other

Focus
- [ ] Cardio
- [ ] Toning
- [ ] Strength
- [ ] Endurance
- [ ] Fitness
- [ ] Maintenance
- [ ] Fat Burn
- [ ] Flexibility
- [ ] Other

Stretch Time

Distance/Steps

Intensity

Day off?	Supplements		Calories Burned	Exercise Mood

Food & Drink

Meal 1:

Time	Mood	Calories

Meal 2:

Time	Mood	Calories

Meal 3:

Time	Mood	Calories

Water & Drinks

Snack:		Snack:	
Time	Calories	Time	Calories

Calories Eaten	Calories Burned	End of day Mood

Summary:

Week 7

Weight		
Neck		
Shoulders		
Chest		
Arms	Left	Right
Waist		
Hips		
Thighs	Left	Right
Calf	Left	Right

Meal Planner

MON	❑ Meal 1	❑ Meal 2	❑ Meal 3
TUE	❑ Meal 1	❑ Meal 2	❑ Meal 3
WED	❑ Meal 1	❑ Meal 2	❑ Meal 3
THU	❑ Meal 1	❑ Meal 2	❑ Meal 3
FRI	❑ Meal 1	❑ Meal 2	❑ Meal 3
SAT	❑ Meal 1	❑ Meal 2	❑ Meal 3
SUN	❑ Meal 1	❑ Meal 2	❑ Meal 3

Exercise

Date:

Exercise	Reps	Sets
1.		
2.		
3.		
4.		
5.		
6.		
7.		
8.		
9.		
10.		

Time

Location

- [ ] Gym
- [ ] Home
- [ ] Outdoors
- [ ] Aquatics
- [ ] Class
- [ ] Other

Focus

- [ ] Cardio
- [ ] Toning
- [ ] Strength
- [ ] Endurance
- [ ] Fitness
- [ ] Maintenance
- [ ] Fat Burn
- [ ] Flexibility
- [ ] Other

Stretch Time

Distance/Steps

Intensity

Day off?	Supplements	Calories Burned	Exercise Mood

Food & Drink

Meal 1:

Time	Mood	Calories

Meal 2:

Time	Mood	Calories

Meal 3:

Time	Mood	Calories

Water & Drinks

Snack:

Snack:

Time	Calories	Time	Calories

Calories Eaten	Calories Burned	End of day Mood

Summary:

Exercise

Date:		
Exercise	**Reps**	**Sets**
1.		
2.		
3.		
4.		
5.		
6.		
7.		
8.		
9.		
10.		

Time

Location

- [ ] Gym
- [ ] Home
- [ ] Outdoors
- [ ] Aquatics
- [ ] Class
- [ ] Other

Focus

- [ ] Cardio
- [ ] Toning
- [ ] Strength
- [ ] Endurance
- [ ] Fitness
- [ ] Maintenance
- [ ] Fat Burn
- [ ] Flexibility
- [ ] Other

Stretch Time

Distance/Steps

Intensity

Day off?	Supplements	Calories Burned	Exercise Mood

Food & Drink

Meal 1:

Time	Mood	Calories

Meal 2:

Time	Mood	Calories

Meal 3:

Time	Mood	Calories

Water & Drinks

Snack:		Snack:	
Time	Calories	Time	Calories

Calories Eaten	Calories Burned	End of day Mood

Summary:

Exercise

Date:

Exercise	Reps	Sets
1.		
2.		
3.		
4.		
5.		
6.		
7.		
8.		
9.		
10.		

Time

Location
- [ ] Gym
- [ ] Home
- [ ] Outdoors
- [ ] Aquatics
- [ ] Class
- [ ] Other

Focus
- [ ] Cardio
- [ ] Toning
- [ ] Strength
- [ ] Endurance
- [ ] Fitness
- [ ] Maintenance
- [ ] Fat Burn
- [ ] Flexibility
- [ ] Other

Stretch Time

Distance/Steps

Intensity

Day off?	Supplements	Calories Burned	Exercise Mood

Food & Drink

Meal 1:

Time	Mood	Calories

Meal 2:

Time	Mood	Calories

Meal 3:

Time	Mood	Calories

Water & Drinks

Snack:

Time	Calories

Snack:

Time	Calories

Calories Eaten	Calories Burned	End of day Mood

Summary:

Exercise

Date:		
Exercise	**Reps**	**Sets**
1.		
2.		
3.		
4.		
5.		
6.		
7.		
8.		
9.		
10.		

Time

Location
- [ ] Gym
- [ ] Home
- [ ] Outdoors
- [ ] Aquatics
- [ ] Class
- [ ] Other

Focus
- [ ] Cardio
- [ ] Toning
- [ ] Strength
- [ ] Endurance
- [ ] Fitness
- [ ] Maintenance
- [ ] Fat Burn
- [ ] Flexibility
- [ ] Other

Stretch Time

Distance/Steps

Intensity

Day off?	Supplements	Calories Burned	Exercise Mood

Food & Drink

Meal 1:

Time	Mood	Calories

Meal 2:

Time	Mood	Calories

Meal 3:

Time	Mood	Calories

Water & Drinks

Snack:

Time	Calories

Snack:

Time	Calories

Calories Eaten	Calories Burned	End of day Mood

Summary:

Exercise

Date:

Exercise	Reps	Sets
1.		
2.		
3.		
4.		
5.		
6.		
7.		
8.		
9.		
10.		

Time

Location
- ☐ Gym
- ☐ Home
- ☐ Outdoors
- ☐ Aquatics
- ☐ Class
- ☐ Other

Focus
- ☐ Cardio
- ☐ Toning
- ☐ Strength
- ☐ Endurance
- ☐ Fitness
- ☐ Maintenance
- ☐ Fat Burn
- ☐ Flexibility
- ☐ Other

Stretch Time

Distance/Steps

Intensity

Day off?	Supplements	Calories Burned	Exercise Mood

Food & Drink

Meal 1:

Time	Mood	Calories

Meal 2:

Time	Mood	Calories

Meal 3:

Time	Mood	Calories

Water & Drinks

Snack:		Snack:	
Time	Calories	Time	Calories

Calories Eaten	Calories Burned	End of day Mood

Summary:

Exercise

Date:

Exercise	Reps	Sets
1.		
2.		
3.		
4.		
5.		
6.		
7.		
8.		
9.		
10.		

Time

Location
- [ ] Gym
- [ ] Home
- [ ] Outdoors
- [ ] Aquatics
- [ ] Class
- [ ] Other

Focus
- [ ] Cardio
- [ ] Toning
- [ ] Strength
- [ ] Endurance
- [ ] Fitness
- [ ] Maintenance
- [ ] Fat Burn
- [ ] Flexibility
- [ ] Other

Stretch Time

Distance/Steps

Intensity

Day off?	Supplements	Calories Burned	Exercise Mood

Food & Drink

Meal 1:

Time	Mood	Calories

Meal 2:

Time	Mood	Calories

Meal 3:

Time	Mood	Calories

Water & Drinks

Snack:

Time	Calories

Snack:

Time	Calories

Calories Eaten	Calories Burned	End of day Mood

Summary:

Exercise

Date:

	Exercise	Reps	Sets
1.			
2.			
3.			
4.			
5.			
6.			
7.			
8.			
9.			
10.			

Time

Location
- [ ] Gym
- [ ] Home
- [ ] Outdoors
- [ ] Aquatics
- [ ] Class
- [ ] Other

Focus
- [ ] Cardio
- [ ] Toning
- [ ] Strength
- [ ] Endurance
- [ ] Fitness
- [ ] Maintenance
- [ ] Fat Burn
- [ ] Flexibility
- [ ] Other

Stretch Time

Distance/Steps

Intensity

Day off?	Supplements	Calories Burned	Exercise Mood

Food & Drink

Meal 1:

Time	Mood	Calories

Meal 2:

Time	Mood	Calories

Meal 3:

Time	Mood	Calories

Water & Drinks

Snack:		Snack:	
Time	Calories	Time	Calories

Calories Eaten	Calories Burned	End of day Mood

Summary:

Week 8

Meal Planner

MON	❑ Meal 1	❑ Meal 2	❑ Meal 3
TUE	❑ Meal 1	❑ Meal 2	❑ Meal 3
WED	❑ Meal 1	❑ Meal 2	❑ Meal 3
THU	❑ Meal 1	❑ Meal 2	❑ Meal 3
FRI	❑ Meal 1	❑ Meal 2	❑ Meal 3
SAT	❑ Meal 1	❑ Meal 2	❑ Meal 3
SUN	❑ Meal 1	❑ Meal 2	❑ Meal 3

Exercise

Date:			
Exercise		**Reps**	**Sets**
1.			
2.			
3.			
4.			
5.			
6.			
7.			
8.			
9.			
10.			

Location

- [ ] Gym
- [ ] Home
- [ ] Outdoors
- [ ] Aquatics
- [ ] Class
- [ ] Other

Focus

- [ ] Cardio
- [ ] Toning
- [ ] Strength
- [ ] Endurance
- [ ] Fitness
- [ ] Maintenance
- [ ] Fat Burn
- [ ] Flexibility
- [ ] Other

Stretch Time

Distance/Steps

Intensity

Day off?	Supplements	Calories Burned	Exercise Mood

Food & Drink

Meal 1:

Time	Mood	Calories

Meal 2:

Time	Mood	Calories

Meal 3:

Time	Mood	Calories

Water & Drinks

Snack:

Time	Calories

Snack:

Time	Calories

Calories Eaten	Calories Burned	End of day Mood

Summary:

Exercise

Date:

Exercise	Reps	Sets
1.		
2.		
3.		
4.		
5.		
6.		
7.		
8.		
9.		
10.		

Time

Location

- [ ] Gym
- [ ] Home
- [ ] Outdoors
- [ ] Aquatics
- [ ] Class
- [ ] Other

Focus

- [ ] Cardio
- [ ] Toning
- [ ] Strength
- [ ] Endurance
- [ ] Fitness
- [ ] Maintenance
- [ ] Fat Burn
- [ ] Flexibility
- [ ] Other

Stretch Time

Distance/Steps

Intensity

Day off?	Supplements	Calories Burned	Exercise Mood

Food & Drink

Meal 1:

Time	Mood	Calories

Meal 2:

Time	Mood	Calories

Meal 3:

Time	Mood	Calories

Water & Drinks

Snack:		Snack:	
Time	Calories	Time	Calories

Calories Eaten	Calories Burned	End of day Mood

Summary:

Exercise

Date:

Exercise	Reps	Sets
1.		
2.		
3.		
4.		
5.		
6.		
7.		
8.		
9.		
10.		

Time

Location

- [ ] Gym
- [ ] Home
- [ ] Outdoors
- [ ] Aquatics
- [ ] Class
- [ ] Other

Focus

- [ ] Cardio
- [ ] Toning
- [ ] Strength
- [ ] Endurance
- [ ] Fitness
- [ ] Maintenance
- [ ] Fat Burn
- [ ] Flexibility
- [ ] Other

Stretch Time

Distance/Steps

Intensity

Day off?	Supplements	Calories Burned	Exercise Mood

Food & Drink

Meal 1:

Time	Mood	Calories

Meal 2:

Time	Mood	Calories

Meal 3:

Time	Mood	Calories

Water & Drinks

Snack:

Time	Calories

Snack:

Time	Calories

Calories Eaten	Calories Burned	End of day Mood

Summary:

Exercise

Date:

Exercise	Reps	Sets
1.		
2.		
3.		
4.		
5.		
6.		
7.		
8.		
9.		
10.		

Time

Location
- ☐ Gym
- ☐ Home
- ☐ Outdoors
- ☐ Aquatics
- ☐ Class
- ☐ Other

Focus
- ☐ Cardio
- ☐ Toning
- ☐ Strength
- ☐ Endurance
- ☐ Fitness
- ☐ Maintenance
- ☐ Fat Burn
- ☐ Flexibility
- ☐ Other

Stretch Time

Distance/Steps

Intensity

Day off?	Supplements	Calories Burned	Exercise Mood

Food & Drink

Meal 1:

Time	Mood	Calories

Meal 2:

Time	Mood	Calories

Meal 3:

Time	Mood	Calories

Water & Drinks

Snack:

Snack:

Time	Calories	Time	Calories

Calories Eaten	Calories Burned	End of day Mood

Summary:

Exercise

Date:

Exercise	Reps	Sets
1.		
2.		
3.		
4.		
5.		
6.		
7.		
8.		
9.		
10.		

Time

Location
- [ ] Gym
- [ ] Home
- [ ] Outdoors
- [ ] Aquatics
- [ ] Class
- [ ] Other

Focus
- [ ] Cardio
- [ ] Toning
- [ ] Strength
- [ ] Endurance
- [ ] Fitness
- [ ] Maintenance
- [ ] Fat Burn
- [ ] Flexibility
- [ ] Other

Stretch Time

Distance/Steps

Intensity

Day off?	Supplements	Calories Burned	Exercise Mood

Food & Drink

Meal 1:

Time	Mood	Calories

Meal 2:

Time	Mood	Calories

Meal 3:

Time	Mood	Calories

Water & Drinks

Snack:

Time	Calories

Snack:

Time	Calories

Calories Eaten	Calories Burned	End of day Mood

Summary:

Exercise

Date:			
Exercise	**Reps**	**Sets**	
1.			
2.			
3.			
4.			
5.			
6.			
7.			
8.			
9.			
10.			

Time

Location
- [ ] Gym
- [ ] Home
- [ ] Outdoors
- [ ] Aquatics
- [ ] Class
- [ ] Other

Focus
- [ ] Cardio
- [ ] Toning
- [ ] Strength
- [ ] Endurance
- [ ] Fitness
- [ ] Maintenance
- [ ] Fat Burn
- [ ] Flexibility
- [ ] Other

Stretch Time

Distance/Steps

Intensity

Day off?	Supplements	Calories Burned	Exercise Mood

Food & Drink

Meal 1:

Time	Mood	Calories

Meal 2:

Time	Mood	Calories

Meal 3:

Time	Mood	Calories

Water & Drinks

Snack:

Snack:

Time	Calories	Time	Calories

Calories Eaten	Calories Burned	End of day Mood

Summary:

Exercise

Date:

Exercise	Reps	Sets
1.		
2.		
3.		
4.		
5.		
6.		
7.		
8.		
9.		
10.		

Location

- [ ] Gym
- [ ] Home
- [ ] Outdoors
- [ ] Aquatics
- [ ] Class
- [ ] Other

Focus

- [ ] Cardio
- [ ] Toning
- [ ] Strength
- [ ] Endurance
- [ ] Fitness
- [ ] Maintenance
- [ ] Fat Burn
- [ ] Flexibility
- [ ] Other

Stretch Time

Distance/Steps

Intensity

Day off?	Supplements	Calories Burned	Exercise Mood

Food & Drink

Meal 1:

Time	Mood	Calories

Meal 2:

Time	Mood	Calories

Meal 3:

Time	Mood	Calories

Water & Drinks

Snack: **Snack:**

Time	Calories	Time	Calories

Calories Eaten	Calories Burned	End of day Mood

Summary:

Week 9

Meal Planner

MON	☐ Meal 1	☐ Meal 2	☐ Meal 3
TUE	☐ Meal 1	☐ Meal 2	☐ Meal 3
WED	☐ Meal 1	☐ Meal 2	☐ Meal 3
THU	☐ Meal 1	☐ Meal 2	☐ Meal 3
FRI	☐ Meal 1	☐ Meal 2	☐ Meal 3
SAT	☐ Meal 1	☐ Meal 2	☐ Meal 3
SUN	☐ Meal 1	☐ Meal 2	☐ Meal 3

Exercise

Date:			
Exercise		**Reps**	**Sets**
1.			
2.			
3.			
4.			
5.			
6.			
7.			
8.			
9.			
10.			

Time

Location
- [ ] Gym
- [ ] Home
- [ ] Outdoors
- [ ] Aquatics
- [ ] Class
- [ ] Other

Focus
- [ ] Cardio
- [ ] Toning
- [ ] Strength
- [ ] Endurance
- [ ] Fitness
- [ ] Maintenance
- [ ] Fat Burn
- [ ] Flexibility
- [ ] Other

Stretch Time

Distance/Steps

Intensity

Day off?	Supplements	Calories Burned	Exercise Mood

Food & Drink

Meal 1:

Time	Mood	Calories

Meal 2:

Time	Mood	Calories

Meal 3:

Time	Mood	Calories

Water & Drinks

Snack:

Time	Calories

Snack:

Time	Calories

Calories Eaten	Calories Burned	End of day Mood

Summary:

Exercise

Date:

Exercise	Reps	Sets
1.		
2.		
3.		
4.		
5.		
6.		
7.		
8.		
9.		
10.		

Time

Location
- [ ] Gym
- [ ] Home
- [ ] Outdoors
- [ ] Aquatics
- [ ] Class
- [ ] Other

Focus
- [ ] Cardio
- [ ] Toning
- [ ] Strength
- [ ] Endurance
- [ ] Fitness
- [ ] Maintenance
- [ ] Fat Burn
- [ ] Flexibility
- [ ] Other

Stretch Time

Distance/Steps

Intensity

Day off?	Supplements	Calories Burned	Exercise Mood

138

Food & Drink

Meal 1:

Time	Mood	Calories

Meal 2:

Time	Mood	Calories

Meal 3:

Time	Mood	Calories

Water & Drinks

Snack:

Snack:

Time	Calories	Time	Calories

Calories Eaten	Calories Burned	End of day Mood

Summary:

Exercise

Date:

Exercise	Reps	Sets
1.		
2.		
3.		
4.		
5.		
6.		
7.		
8.		
9.		
10.		

Time

Location
- [ ] Gym
- [ ] Home
- [ ] Outdoors
- [ ] Aquatics
- [ ] Class
- [ ] Other

Focus
- [ ] Cardio
- [ ] Toning
- [ ] Strength
- [ ] Endurance
- [ ] Fitness
- [ ] Maintenance
- [ ] Fat Burn
- [ ] Flexibility
- [ ] Other

Stretch Time

Distance/Steps

Intensity

Day off?	Supplements	Calories Burned	Exercise Mood

Food & Drink

Meal 1:

Time	Mood	Calories

Meal 2:

Time	Mood	Calories

Meal 3:

Time	Mood	Calories

Water & Drinks

Snack:

Time	Calories

Snack:

Time	Calories

Calories Eaten	Calories Burned	End of day Mood

Summary:

Exercise

Date:

Exercise	Reps	Sets
1.		
2.		
3.		
4.		
5.		
6.		
7.		
8.		
9.		
10.		

Time

Location

- [ ] Gym
- [ ] Home
- [ ] Outdoors
- [ ] Aquatics
- [ ] Class
- [ ] Other

Focus

- [ ] Cardio
- [ ] Toning
- [ ] Strength
- [ ] Endurance
- [ ] Fitness
- [ ] Maintenance
- [ ] Fat Burn
- [ ] Flexibility
- [ ] Other

Stretch Time

Distance/Steps

Intensity

Day off?	Supplements	Calories Burned	Exercise Mood

Food & Drink

Meal 1:

Time	Mood	Calories

Meal 2:

Time	Mood	Calories

Meal 3:

Time	Mood	Calories

Water & Drinks

Snack:		Snack:	
Time	Calories	Time	Calories

Calories Eaten	Calories Burned	End of day Mood

Summary:

Exercise

Date:

Exercise	Reps	Sets
1.		
2.		
3.		
4.		
5.		
6.		
7.		
8.		
9.		
10.		

Time

Location
- [ ] Gym
- [ ] Home
- [ ] Outdoors
- [ ] Aquatics
- [ ] Class
- [ ] Other

Focus
- [ ] Cardio
- [ ] Toning
- [ ] Strength
- [ ] Endurance
- [ ] Fitness
- [ ] Maintenance
- [ ] Fat Burn
- [ ] Flexibility
- [ ] Other

Stretch Time

Distance/Steps

Intensity

Day off?	Supplements	Calories Burned	Exercise Mood

Food & Drink

Meal 1:

Time	Mood	Calories

Meal 2:

Time	Mood	Calories

Meal 3:

Time	Mood	Calories

Water & Drinks

Snack:

Time	Calories

Snack:

Time	Calories

Calories Eaten	Calories Burned	End of day Mood

Summary:

Exercise

Date:

Exercise	Reps	Sets
1.		
2.		
3.		
4.		
5.		
6.		
7.		
8.		
9.		
10.		

Time

Location
- [ ] Gym
- [ ] Home
- [ ] Outdoors
- [ ] Aquatics
- [ ] Class
- [ ] Other

Focus
- [ ] Cardio
- [ ] Toning
- [ ] Strength
- [ ] Endurance
- [ ] Fitness
- [ ] Maintenance
- [ ] Fat Burn
- [ ] Flexibility
- [ ] Other

Stretch Time

Distance/Steps

Intensity

Day off?	Supplements	Calories Burned	Exercise Mood

Food & Drink

Meal 1:

Time	Mood	Calories

Meal 2:

Time	Mood	Calories

Meal 3:

Time	Mood	Calories

Water & Drinks

Snack:

Snack:

Time	Calories	Time	Calories

Calories Eaten	Calories Burned	End of day Mood

Summary:

_____

_____

_____

_____

Exercise

Date:

Exercise	Reps	Sets
1.		
2.		
3.		
4.		
5.		
6.		
7.		
8.		
9.		
10.		

Time

Location
- [ ] Gym
- [ ] Home
- [ ] Outdoors
- [ ] Aquatics
- [ ] Class
- [ ] Other

Focus
- [ ] Cardio
- [ ] Toning
- [ ] Strength
- [ ] Endurance
- [ ] Fitness
- [ ] Maintenance
- [ ] Fat Burn
- [ ] Flexibility
- [ ] Other

Stretch Time

Distance/Steps

Intensity

Day off?	Supplements	Calories Burned	Exercise Mood

Food & Drink

Meal 1:

Time	Mood	Calories

Meal 2:

Time	Mood	Calories

Meal 3:

Time	Mood	Calories

Water & Drinks

Snack:		Snack:	
Time	Calories	Time	Calories

Calories Eaten	Calories Burned	End of day Mood

Summary:

Week 10

Weight		
Neck		
Shoulders		
Chest		
Arms	Left	Right
Waist		
Hips		
Thighs	Left	Right
Calf	Left	Right

Meal Planner

MON	☐ Meal 1	☐ Meal 2	☐ Meal 3
TUE	☐ Meal 1	☐ Meal 2	☐ Meal 3
WED	☐ Meal 1	☐ Meal 2	☐ Meal 3
THU	☐ Meal 1	☐ Meal 2	☐ Meal 3
FRI	☐ Meal 1	☐ Meal 2	☐ Meal 3
SAT	☐ Meal 1	☐ Meal 2	☐ Meal 3
SUN	☐ Meal 1	☐ Meal 2	☐ Meal 3

Exercise

Date:

	Exercise	Reps	Sets
1.			
2.			
3.			
4.			
5.			
6.			
7.			
8.			
9.			
10.			

Time

Location

- ☐ Gym
- ☐ Home
- ☐ Outdoors
- ☐ Aquatics
- ☐ Class
- ☐ Other

Focus

- ☐ Cardio
- ☐ Toning
- ☐ Strength
- ☐ Endurance
- ☐ Fitness
- ☐ Maintenance
- ☐ Fat Burn
- ☐ Flexibility
- ☐ Other

Stretch Time

Distance/Steps

Intensity

Day off?	Supplements	Calories Burned	Exercise Mood

Food & Drink

Meal 1:

Time	Mood	Calories

Meal 2:

Time	Mood	Calories

Meal 3:

Time	Mood	Calories

Water & Drinks

Snack:		Snack:	
Time	Calories	Time	Calories

Calories Eaten	Calories Burned	End of day Mood

Summary:

Exercise

Date: _____

Exercise	Reps	Sets
1.		
2.		
3.		
4.		
5.		
6.		
7.		
8.		
9.		
10.		

Time

Location
- [ ] Gym
- [ ] Home
- [ ] Outdoors
- [ ] Aquatics
- [ ] Class
- [ ] Other

Focus
- [ ] Cardio
- [ ] Toning
- [ ] Strength
- [ ] Endurance
- [ ] Fitness
- [ ] Maintenance
- [ ] Fat Burn
- [ ] Flexibility
- [ ] Other

Stretch Time

Distance/Steps

Intensity

Day off?	Supplements	Calories Burned	Exercise Mood

Food & Drink

Meal 1:

Time	Mood	Calories

Meal 2:

Time	Mood	Calories

Meal 3:

Time	Mood	Calories

Water & Drinks

Snack:

Snack:

Time	Calories	Time	Calories

Calories Eaten	Calories Burned	End of day Mood

Summary:

Exercise

Date:

Exercise	Reps	Sets
1.		
2.		
3.		
4.		
5.		
6.		
7.		
8.		
9.		
10.		

Location

- [ ] Gym
- [ ] Home
- [ ] Outdoors
- [ ] Aquatics
- [ ] Class
- [ ] Other

Focus

- [ ] Cardio
- [ ] Toning
- [ ] Strength
- [ ] Endurance
- [ ] Fitness
- [ ] Maintenance
- [ ] Fat Burn
- [ ] Flexibility
- [ ] Other

Stretch Time

Distance/Steps

Intensity

Day off?	Supplements	Calories Burned	Exercise Mood

Food & Drink

Meal 1:

Time	Mood	Calories

Meal 2:

Time	Mood	Calories

Meal 3:

Time	Mood	Calories

Water & Drinks

Snack:		Snack:	
Time	Calories	Time	Calories

Calories Eaten	Calories Burned	End of day Mood

Summary:

Exercise

Date:

Exercise	Reps	Sets
1.		
2.		
3.		
4.		
5.		
6.		
7.		
8.		
9.		
10.		

Time

Location

- [ ] Gym
- [ ] Home
- [ ] Outdoors
- [ ] Aquatics
- [ ] Class
- [ ] Other

Focus

- [ ] Cardio
- [ ] Toning
- [ ] Strength
- [ ] Endurance
- [ ] Fitness
- [ ] Maintenance
- [ ] Fat Burn
- [ ] Flexibility
- [ ] Other

Stretch Time

Distance/Steps

Intensity

Day off?	Supplements	Calories Burned	Exercise Mood

Food & Drink

Meal 1:

Time	Mood	Calories

Meal 2:

Time	Mood	Calories

Meal 3:

Time	Mood	Calories

Snack:		Snack:	
Time	Calories	Time	Calories

Water & Drinks

Calories Eaten	Calories Burned	End of day Mood

Summary:

Exercise

Date:

Exercise	Reps	Sets
1.		
2.		
3.		
4.		
5.		
6.		
7.		
8.		
9.		
10.		

Time

Location
- [ ] Gym
- [ ] Home
- [ ] Outdoors
- [ ] Aquatics
- [ ] Class
- [ ] Other

Focus
- [ ] Cardio
- [ ] Toning
- [ ] Strength
- [ ] Endurance
- [ ] Fitness
- [ ] Maintenance
- [ ] Fat Burn
- [ ] Flexibility
- [ ] Other

Stretch Time

Distance/Steps

Intensity

Day off?	Supplements	Calories Burned	Exercise Mood

Food & Drink

Meal 1:

Time	Mood	Calories

Meal 2:

Time	Mood	Calories

Meal 3:

Time	Mood	Calories

Water & Drinks

Snack:

Time	Calories

Snack:

Time	Calories

Calories Eaten	Calories Burned	End of day Mood

Summary:

_____

_____

_____

Exercise

Date:

Exercise	Reps	Sets
1.		
2.		
3.		
4.		
5.		
6.		
7.		
8.		
9.		
10.		

Time

Location
- [ ] Gym
- [ ] Home
- [ ] Outdoors
- [ ] Aquatics
- [ ] Class
- [ ] Other

Focus
- [ ] Cardio
- [ ] Toning
- [ ] Strength
- [ ] Endurance
- [ ] Fitness
- [ ] Maintenance
- [ ] Fat Burn
- [ ] Flexibility
- [ ] Other

Stretch Time

Distance/Steps

Intensity

Day off?	Supplements	Calories Burned	Exercise Mood

Food & Drink

Meal 1:

Time	Mood	Calories

Meal 2:

Time	Mood	Calories

Meal 3:

Time	Mood	Calories

Water & Drinks

Snack:

Time	Calories

Snack:

Time	Calories

Calories Eaten	Calories Burned	End of day Mood

Summary:

Exercise

Date:

Exercise	Reps	Sets
1.		
2.		
3.		
4.		
5.		
6.		
7.		
8.		
9.		
10.		

Time

Location

- [ ] Gym
- [ ] Home
- [ ] Outdoors
- [ ] Aquatics
- [ ] Class
- [ ] Other

Focus

- [ ] Cardio
- [ ] Toning
- [ ] Strength
- [ ] Endurance
- [ ] Fitness
- [ ] Maintenance
- [ ] Fat Burn
- [ ] Flexibility
- [ ] Other

Stretch Time

Distance/Steps

Intensity

Day off?	Supplements	Calories Burned	Exercise Mood

Food & Drink

Meal 1:

Time	Mood	Calories

Meal 2:

Time	Mood	Calories

Meal 3:

Time	Mood	Calories

Water & Drinks

Snack:

Time	Calories

Snack:

Time	Calories

Calories Eaten	Calories Burned	End of day Mood

Summary:

Week 11

Meal Planner

MON	❑ Meal 1	❑ Meal 2	❑ Meal 3
TUE	❑ Meal 1	❑ Meal 2	❑ Meal 3
WED	❑ Meal 1	❑ Meal 2	❑ Meal 3
THU	❑ Meal 1	❑ Meal 2	❑ Meal 3
FRI	❑ Meal 1	❑ Meal 2	❑ Meal 3
SAT	❑ Meal 1	❑ Meal 2	❑ Meal 3
SUN	❑ Meal 1	❑ Meal 2	❑ Meal 3

Exercise

Date:

Exercise	Reps	Sets
1.		
2.		
3.		
4.		
5.		
6.		
7.		
8.		
9.		
10.		

Time

Location
- [ ] Gym
- [ ] Home
- [ ] Outdoors
- [ ] Aquatics
- [ ] Class
- [ ] Other

Focus
- [ ] Cardio
- [ ] Toning
- [ ] Strength
- [ ] Endurance
- [ ] Fitness
- [ ] Maintenance
- [ ] Fat Burn
- [ ] Flexibility
- [ ] Other

Stretch Time

Distance/Steps

Intensity

Day off?	Supplements	Calories Burned	Exercise Mood

Food & Drink

Meal 1:

Time	Mood	Calories

Meal 2:

Time	Mood	Calories

Meal 3:

Time	Mood	Calories

Water & Drinks

Snack:

Snack:

Time	Calories	Time	Calories

Calories Eaten	Calories Burned	End of day Mood

Summary:

Exercise

Date:

Exercise	Reps	Sets
1.		
2.		
3.		
4.		
5.		
6.		
7.		
8.		
9.		
10.		

Time

Location

- ☐ Gym
- ☐ Home
- ☐ Outdoors
- ☐ Aquatics
- ☐ Class
- ☐ Other

Focus

- ☐ Cardio
- ☐ Toning
- ☐ Strength
- ☐ Endurance
- ☐ Fitness
- ☐ Maintenance
- ☐ Fat Burn
- ☐ Flexibility
- ☐ Other

Stretch Time

Distance/Steps

Intensity

Day off?	Supplements	Calories Burned	Exercise Mood

Food & Drink

Meal 1:

Time	Mood	Calories

Meal 2:

Time	Mood	Calories

Meal 3:

Time	Mood	Calories

Water & Drinks

Snack:		Snack:	
Time	Calories	Time	Calories

Calories Eaten	Calories Burned	End of day Mood

Summary:

Exercise

Date:

Exercise	Reps	Sets
1.		
2.		
3.		
4.		
5.		
6.		
7.		
8.		
9.		
10.		

Time

Location

- [ ] Gym
- [ ] Home
- [ ] Outdoors
- [ ] Aquatics
- [ ] Class
- [ ] Other

Focus

- [ ] Cardio
- [ ] Toning
- [ ] Strength
- [ ] Endurance
- [ ] Fitness
- [ ] Maintenance
- [ ] Fat Burn
- [ ] Flexibility
- [ ] Other

Stretch Time

Distance/Steps

Intensity

Day off?	Supplements	Calories Burned	Exercise Mood

Food & Drink

Meal 1:

Time	Mood	Calories

Meal 2:

Time	Mood	Calories

Meal 3:

Time	Mood	Calories

Water & Drinks

Snack:

Time	Calories

Snack:

Time	Calories

Calories Eaten	Calories Burned	End of day Mood

Summary:

_____

_____

_____

Exercise

Date:

Exercise	Reps	Sets
1.		
2.		
3.		
4.		
5.		
6.		
7.		
8.		
9.		
10.		

Location

- ☐ Gym
- ☐ Home
- ☐ Outdoors
- ☐ Aquatics
- ☐ Class
- ☐ Other

Focus

- ☐ Cardio
- ☐ Toning
- ☐ Strength
- ☐ Endurance
- ☐ Fitness
- ☐ Maintenance
- ☐ Fat Burn
- ☐ Flexibility
- ☐ Other

Stretch Time

Distance/Steps

Intensity

Day off?	Supplements	Calories Burned	Exercise Mood

Food & Drink

Meal 1:

Time	Mood	Calories

Meal 2:

Time	Mood	Calories

Meal 3:

Time	Mood	Calories

Water & Drinks

Snack:

Time	Calories

Snack:

Time	Calories

Calories Eaten	Calories Burned	End of day Mood

Summary:

Exercise

Date:

Exercise	Reps	Sets
1.		
2.		
3.		
4.		
5.		
6.		
7.		
8.		
9.		
10.		

Time

Location
- [ ] Gym
- [ ] Home
- [ ] Outdoors
- [ ] Aquatics
- [ ] Class
- [ ] Other

Focus
- [ ] Cardio
- [ ] Toning
- [ ] Strength
- [ ] Endurance
- [ ] Fitness
- [ ] Maintenance
- [ ] Fat Burn
- [ ] Flexibility
- [ ] Other

Stretch Time

Distance/Steps

Intensity

Day off?	Supplements	Calories Burned	Exercise Mood

Food & Drink

Meal 1:

Time	Mood	Calories

Meal 2:

Time	Mood	Calories

Meal 3:

Time	Mood	Calories

Water & Drinks

Snack:

Snack:

Time	Calories	Time	Calories

Calories Eaten	Calories Burned	End of day Mood

Summary:

Exercise

Date:			
Exercise		**Reps**	**Sets**
1.			
2.			
3.			
4.			
5.			
6.			
7.			
8.			
9.			
10.			

Time

Location
- [ ] Gym
- [ ] Home
- [ ] Outdoors
- [ ] Aquatics
- [ ] Class
- [ ] Other

Focus
- [ ] Cardio
- [ ] Toning
- [ ] Strength
- [ ] Endurance
- [ ] Fitness
- [ ] Maintenance
- [ ] Fat Burn
- [ ] Flexibility
- [ ] Other

Stretch Time

Distance/Steps

Intensity

Day off?	Supplements	Calories Burned	Exercise Mood

Food & Drink

Meal 1:

Time	Mood	Calories

Meal 2:

Time	Mood	Calories

Meal 3:

Time	Mood	Calories

Water & Drinks

Snack:		Snack:	
Time	Calories	Time	Calories

Calories Eaten	Calories Burned	End of day Mood

Summary:

Exercise

Date:

Exercise	Reps	Sets
1.		
2.		
3.		
4.		
5.		
6.		
7.		
8.		
9.		
10.		

Time

Location

- [ ] Gym
- [ ] Home
- [ ] Outdoors
- [ ] Aquatics
- [ ] Class
- [ ] Other

Focus

- [ ] Cardio
- [ ] Toning
- [ ] Strength
- [ ] Endurance
- [ ] Fitness
- [ ] Maintenance
- [ ] Fat Burn
- [ ] Flexibility
- [ ] Other

Stretch Time

Distance/Steps

Intensity

Day off?	Supplements	Calories Burned	Exercise Mood

Food & Drink

Meal 1:

Time	Mood	Calories

Meal 2:

Time	Mood	Calories

Meal 3:

Time	Mood	Calories

Water & Drinks

Snack:		Snack:	
Time	Calories	Time	Calories

Calories Eaten	Calories Burned	End of day Mood

Summary:

Week 12

Meal Planner

MON	❏ Meal 1 ❏ Meal 2 ❏ Meal 3
TUE	❏ Meal 1 ❏ Meal 2 ❏ Meal 3
WED	❏ Meal 1 ❏ Meal 2 ❏ Meal 3
THU	❏ Meal 1 ❏ Meal 2 ❏ Meal 3
FRI	❏ Meal 1 ❏ Meal 2 ❏ Meal 3
SAT	❏ Meal 1 ❏ Meal 2 ❏ Meal 3
SUN	❏ Meal 1 ❏ Meal 2 ❏ Meal 3

Exercise

Date:		
Exercise	**Reps**	**Sets**
1.		
2.		
3.		
4.		
5.		
6.		
7.		
8.		
9.		
10.		

Time

Location

- ☐ Gym
- ☐ Home
- ☐ Outdoors
- ☐ Aquatics
- ☐ Class
- ☐ Other

Focus

- ☐ Cardio
- ☐ Toning
- ☐ Strength
- ☐ Endurance
- ☐ Fitness
- ☐ Maintenance
- ☐ Fat Burn
- ☐ Flexibility
- ☐ Other

Stretch Time

Distance/Steps

Intensity

Day off?	Supplements	Calories Burned	Exercise Mood

Food & Drink

Meal 1:

Time	Mood	Calories

Meal 2:

Time	Mood	Calories

Meal 3:

Time	Mood	Calories

Water & Drinks

Snack:

Time	Calories

Snack:

Time	Calories

Calories Eaten	Calories Burned	End of day Mood

Summary:

Exercise

Date:

Exercise	Reps	Sets
1.		
2.		
3.		
4.		
5.		
6.		
7.		
8.		
9.		
10.		

Time

Location

- [ ] Gym
- [ ] Home
- [ ] Outdoors
- [ ] Aquatics
- [ ] Class
- [ ] Other

Focus

- [ ] Cardio
- [ ] Toning
- [ ] Strength
- [ ] Endurance
- [ ] Fitness
- [ ] Maintenance
- [ ] Fat Burn
- [ ] Flexibility
- [ ] Other

Stretch Time

Distance/Steps

Intensity

Day off?	Supplements	Calories Burned	Exercise Mood

Food & Drink

Meal 1:

Time	Mood	Calories

Meal 2:

Time	Mood	Calories

Meal 3:

Time	Mood	Calories

Water & Drinks

Snack:

Time	Calories

Snack:

Time	Calories

Calories Eaten	Calories Burned	End of day Mood

Summary:

_____

_____

_____

Exercise

Date:

Exercise	Reps	Sets
1.		
2.		
3.		
4.		
5.		
6.		
7.		
8.		
9.		
10.		

Time

Location

- [ ] Gym
- [ ] Home
- [ ] Outdoors
- [ ] Aquatics
- [ ] Class
- [ ] Other

Focus

- [ ] Cardio
- [ ] Toning
- [ ] Strength
- [ ] Endurance
- [ ] Fitness
- [ ] Maintenance
- [ ] Fat Burn
- [ ] Flexibility
- [ ] Other

Stretch Time

Distance/Steps

Intensity

Day off?	Supplements	Calories Burned	Exercise Mood

Food & Drink

Meal 1:

Time	Mood	Calories

Meal 2:

Time	Mood	Calories

Meal 3:

Time	Mood	Calories

Water & Drinks

Snack:		Snack:	
Time	Calories	Time	Calories

Calories Eaten	Calories Burned	End of day Mood

Summary:

Exercise

Date:

Exercise	Reps	Sets
1.		
2.		
3.		
4.		
5.		
6.		
7.		
8.		
9.		
10.		

Time

Location

- ☐ Gym
- ☐ Home
- ☐ Outdoors
- ☐ Aquatics
- ☐ Class
- ☐ Other

Focus

- ☐ Cardio
- ☐ Toning
- ☐ Strength
- ☐ Endurance
- ☐ Fitness
- ☐ Maintenance
- ☐ Fat Burn
- ☐ Flexibility
- ☐ Other

Stretch Time

Distance/Steps

Intensity

Day off?	Supplements	Calories Burned	Exercise Mood

Food & Drink

Meal 1:

Time	Mood	Calories

Meal 2:

Time	Mood	Calories

Meal 3:

Time	Mood	Calories

Water & Drinks

Snack: | **Snack:**

Time	Calories	Time	Calories

Calories Eaten	Calories Burned	End of day Mood

Summary:

_____

_____

_____

Exercise

Date:

Exercise	Reps	Sets
1.		
2.		
3.		
4.		
5.		
6.		
7.		
8.		
9.		
10.		

Time

Location
- [ ] Gym
- [ ] Home
- [ ] Outdoors
- [ ] Aquatics
- [ ] Class
- [ ] Other

Focus
- [ ] Cardio
- [ ] Toning
- [ ] Strength
- [ ] Endurance
- [ ] Fitness
- [ ] Maintenance
- [ ] Fat Burn
- [ ] Flexibility
- [ ] Other

Stretch Time

Distance/Steps

Intensity

Day off?	Supplements	Calories Burned	Exercise Mood

Food & Drink

Meal 1:

Time	Mood	Calories

Meal 2:

Time	Mood	Calories

Meal 3:

Time	Mood	Calories

Water & Drinks

Snack:

Time	Calories

Snack:

Time	Calories

Calories Eaten	Calories Burned	End of day Mood

Summary:

_____

_____

_____

_____

Exercise

Date:

Exercise	Reps	Sets
1.		
2.		
3.		
4.		
5.		
6.		
7.		
8.		
9.		
10.		

Time

Location

- [ ] Gym
- [ ] Home
- [ ] Outdoors
- [ ] Aquatics
- [ ] Class
- [ ] Other

Focus

- [ ] Cardio
- [ ] Toning
- [ ] Strength
- [ ] Endurance
- [ ] Fitness
- [ ] Maintenance
- [ ] Fat Burn
- [ ] Flexibility
- [ ] Other

Stretch Time

Distance/Steps

Intensity

Day off?	Supplements	Calories Burned	Exercise Mood

Food & Drink

Meal 1:

Time	Mood	Calories

Meal 2:

Time	Mood	Calories

Meal 3:

Time	Mood	Calories

Water & Drinks

Snack:

Time	Calories

Snack:

Time	Calories

Calories Eaten	Calories Burned	End of day Mood

Summary:

Exercise

Date:

Exercise	Reps	Sets
1.		
2.		
3.		
4.		
5.		
6.		
7.		
8.		
9.		
10.		

Time

Location

- [ ] Gym
- [ ] Home
- [ ] Outdoors
- [ ] Aquatics
- [ ] Class
- [ ] Other

Focus

- [ ] Cardio
- [ ] Toning
- [ ] Strength
- [ ] Endurance
- [ ] Fitness
- [ ] Maintenance
- [ ] Fat Burn
- [ ] Flexibility
- [ ] Other

Stretch Time

Distance/Steps

Intensity

Day off?	Supplements	Calories Burned	Exercise Mood

Food & Drink

Meal 1:

Time	Mood	Calories

Meal 2:

Time	Mood	Calories

Meal 3:

Time	Mood	Calories

Water & Drinks

Snack:		Snack:	
Time	Calories	Time	Calories

Calories Eaten	Calories Burned	End of day Mood

Summary:

Final Result

Weight		Loss

Neck		Loss
Shoulders		Loss
Chest		Loss
Arms	Left	Right	Loss
Waist		Loss
Hips		Loss
Thighs	Left	Right	Loss
Calf	Left	Right	Loss
Total Loss Results:		

Notes

Printed in Great Britain
by Amazon

79484541R00115